REFUSE TO GIVE UP

CRUSH YOUR FEARS AND LIMITING BELIEFS

& DESIGN THE INCREDIBLE LIFE YOU DESERVE!

Henry M. Kaminski Jr.

Copyright © 2016 Higher Purpose Publishing a Division of Marketing Huddle, LLC

ISBN-10: 1539039854

ALL RIGHTS RESERVED. No part of this book may be reproduced or transmitted in any form whatsoever, electronic, or mechanical, including photocopying, recording, or by any informational storage or retrieval system without express written, dated and signed permission from the author.

DISCLAIMER AND/OR LEGAL NOTICES: The information presented in this report represents the views of the publisher as of the date of publication. The publisher reserves the rights to alter and update their opinions based on new conditions. This book is for informational purposes only. The author and the publisher do not accept any responsibilities for any liabilities resulting from the use of this information. While every attempt has been made to verify the information provided here, the author and the publisher cannot assume any responsibility for errors, inaccuracies or omissions. Any similarities with people or facts are unintentional.

Manufactured & Printed in the United States of America.

Henry M. Kaminski, Jr. | Founder | Unique Designz

It all started with a strong work ethic and "never give up" attitude.

Learn how Henry Kaminski Jr., CEO of Unique Designz, a boutique graphic design and marketing firm, began his entrepreneurial journey to becoming a "Million Dollar Designer."

To call Unique Designz's clientele diverse is an understatement; from small, home-based businesses to the Bon Jovi fan club, Kaminski has helped countless businesses increase their exposure, profitability, and brand identity. In 2009, Kaminski was commissioned to design the Backstage with Jon Bon Jovi album cover for the official Jon Bon Jovi fan club, as well as create marketing collateral for Bon Jovi's world tour.

Kaminski's greatest asset is his ability to develop and sustain solid relationships with his clients, and he pours his heart, soul and dedication into each marketing piece that he creates.

Table of Contents

Introduction 1
Interview with Henry M. Kaminski Jr. 3
DESIGN APPLICATION #1 What's Your "WHY?" 17
DESIGN PRINCIPLE #2 23
DESIGN APPLICATION #2 27
DESIGN PRINCIPLE #3 29
DESIGN APPLICATION #3 36
DESIGN PRINCIPLE #4 44
DESIGN APPLICATION #4 51
Connect with Henry 59

Introduction

I want to start by thanking you for giving me the opportunity to tell my life's story. This book touches upon four guiding principles that have helped me grow my business significantly, and my hope is that after reading, you are able to implement these principles. This book has two unique aspects: First, it was written as an interview so that you feel as if I am speaking directly to you. I've also strategically placed workbook pages so that you can record your own thoughts as you read, because in order for you to be able to implement these principles, you must first understand them. My hope is that you come away from this experience with a dramatic shift in your outlook on both your personal and professional life the same way that I did.

Henry M. Kaminski Jr.

This book is dedicated to my beautiful wife for being my guiding light, always supporting me in good times and in bad, and for loving me unconditionally.

I also dedicate this book to my father for always pushing me to be the best in everything that I do and instilling the "refuse to give up" mentality that has made me the man I am today. Thank you for dedicating your life to raising me; you are my super hero and I am blessed to have you as my dad.

Refuse to Give Up

Interview with Henry M. Kaminski Jr.

Tell me about your background and what makes your company, Unique Designz so "unique."

Henry: Unique Designz was formed about nine years ago, sort of by accident quite frankly. My first job out of college was as a same day surgery registrar at a local hospital. I was responsible for making sure that someone coming in for surgery was scheduled correctly; a very mundane job, but something that I needed to do because I had bills to pay. I was so eager to get out into the workforce and building a career that I took the first job I could get my hands on not really thinking about whether it would fulfill me or not. I spent half of my day cleaning coffee pots- it was terrible, and I said you know what, after getting a college degree, this is all that I could come up with? I just couldn't settle for that.

From there, I applied to every job at the hospital that interested me. But, over, and over and over again I would get denied, due to a lack of experience or simply not being the "right fit." It drove me crazy. Finally, about five years later, I landed a position as a Special Events Director at the Children's Hospital. I was responsible for creating events to raise money for Sudden Infant Death Syndrome (SIDS). If you don't know what SIDS is, it's when a baby under the age of one dies unexpectedly without any cause of death. This was an extremely challenging role because it was a difficult charity to raise money for; people had a hard time donating when there were no answers as to what caused SIDS.

After two years, I landed a sponsorship from Z100 radio-the biggest radio station in New York City. When I asked if they would sponsor my event, they said "yes, absolutely," and they welcomed the opportunity with open arms. They even sent

Danielle Monaro from the morning show out to the event. Super cool stuff. I knew that this was my one shot to really shine and wanted to really promote the event with tons of marketing materials, flyers, brochures, posters, you name it.

My buddy Jerry Cammarota, who was a graphic designer, donated all of the marketing materials for the event. I sat down with him to map out the campaign, and was enamored by his ability to design things; I loved learning about graphic design and was immediately fascinated, so much so that I wanted to learn how to design. The event ended up being a huge success, and we raised thousands of dollars. I was psyched and knew that I wanted to learn graphic design, so I convinced my boss at the time to invest in Photoshop so that I could do all of the in-house design on my own. It wasn't before long that people were asking me who was doing the design work for our department, and I said, "well I am."

As I got better at designing, I started to build up a small client base outside of the hospital. I had no formal training, but a real passion for what I was doing, and one client, would become two, three, four… I spent hours each day sitting on a bar stool at my counter studying YouTube tutorials on how to use Photoshop. I had no money at the time, and didn't even have an external mouse to plug into my computer; I literally used my finger on the tiny mouse pad to do my work. In 2009, there was a big shake up at the hospital, and people started getting laid off. At that time, half of my salary was funded by a grant and I was told by my boss that effective January 1st the grant was going away. I could either stay making half the salary or leave. This was at the same time that I was getting ready to propose to my then girlfriend.

I was getting better at designing, but still feeling trapped in what I felt was a "dead end" day job, and I had to make a choice. My boss came back to me and asked if I wanted to stay on board, keeping my benefits but collecting a lower pay, or leave. I thought about it for a second, and said, "you know what, I have to do what my heart tells me," and so I left.

I had started Unique Designz as a side gig about a year prior, but I knew that when I left the hospital, I had no choice but to grow my design business and take it full time. I established Unique Designz as an LLC in 2010, and generated nearly $250K in revenue my first year in business.

Who do you have the most passion for helping?

Henry: At the end of the day we only have one "at bat" in this game of life. When I see people going above and beyond to truly make their lives the best that it can be, while at the same time helping others, that's who I want to help. And I don't just mean financially. I used to be motivated by the wrong things, which I'll get into later, but now I am at a place where I am motivated by the motivation of others.

That takes it past: "I help doctors, lawyers, chiropractors, construction workers" to a higher level; it sounds like you actually want to help people make a real difference in the world.

Henry: That's the big picture. I have a soft spot in my heart for the person who created their business from scratch like I did.
I really want to help that person, and share my experiences with them, so that they can get to the level that I'm at today. Any entrepreneur will tell you, there's no straight road to success; there will constantly be peaks and valleys, so if I can help them get to a better place-more profitable place- faster than I did, and without making the same mistakes that I did, I will feel as if I have succeeded.

Our company is much more than just a design firm; I have learned to shift my creativity from just designing marketing collateral to really helping my clients grow their own businesses beyond the marketing and that's rare. Not a lot of graphic designers have a keen business sense, and that's something that I pride myself on. It wasn't always that way, but now we operate as a one stop shop where a client can boost their marketing in the short term, while also growing their business in the longer term. The question I ask myself before I onboard a new client is:

Henry M. Kaminski Jr.

"How can I use my God-given abilities to help this person grow their own business?" Bottom line.

One of the things that you mentioned is having no formal training. Some people could view this as a negative, but because you look at things through a different lense, it sounds as if you are a proponent of learning from your mistakes. Is that an accurate description?

Henry: Yeah, I sure am. Listen, nobody's perfect, and the only way to learn is to learn is to make mistakes. I'm a real fan of John Maxwell's book "Failing Forward," because nothing resonates with me more than understanding how we can learn, grow, and expand without making mistakes- if we're not failing. So many people are afraid of failure. But, if you just come to terms with what the worst case scenario might be if you do fail, and are willing to accept it, that failure doesn't seem so bad. What's the worst that could happen?

Let's talk about your four guiding principles for success, which are: what's your WHY, having a vision, things aren't always what they seem, and building relationships. How did you come up with these?

Henry: I struggled a lot in the beginning as I was launching Unique Designz full time because I really didn't know what my "why" was. As I grew the business and matured as a person, I learned that things really aren't what they seem; I saw things go down in my own life that proved this. I finally took a step back one day, and said "whoa, money isn't the cure." I've known people with a ton of money who I thought were happy just to find out that they were really in a dark, dark place. As far as building relationships go, life is all about the relationships that we make, because you can't get through life without them. That principle is about building the right relationships-and them continuing to nurture them.

Do you feel that it was a culmination of events in your life that allowed you to bring the whole picture into focus? Can you think of any trigger events that might have made you really sit up and take notice of a life lesson?

Henry: There were a couple of things that happened, which I call benchmarks. But, the real catalyst was in the fourth grade. What happened then sort of triggered everything else. It's funny, I always had trouble reading, and hated reading in front of people. You know how when you're in school and the teacher makes the class each take a sentence or a paragraph to read? Well it was a really emotional time for me, as my parents were going through a nasty divorce; I mean the worst, and I was seeing things at home that no kid should ever have to see. I was having a really bad day, and my teacher called on me to read out loud. I remember looking up at my teacher after she called my name, and then immediately putting my head back down towards my desk hoping that she would skip over me. She called on me again, and I looked up and was just like, "I can't do this," and I started to cry. She didn't know what was going on at home, and told me to step outside. She asked me what was wrong, and I told her about my parents divorcing, and she kind of just smiled. We walked back into class and she told the other kids to close their books. She said, "we're not going to do anymore reading today. We're going to help Henry." She tried to explain to the class what was going on with me-but remember, we were eight-nine years old, and most kids didn't even know what divorce was. She went into this whole thing about relationships and divorce – the whole nine – it was crazy. Then, one by one kids started raising their hands saying that their parents were also getting divorced. I remember one kid saying "I'm going through the same thing you are Henry. Maybe I can help you." We all started sharing our stories with one another —it was a pretty powerful moment for me.

Then, right before the class ended, something strange happened. I found myself in the back of the classroom near the coat closet giving other kids advice. I went from needing the help, to helping them. I still remember what I felt like at that moment to help those kids. I was the one raising my hand screaming for help and by the end of the class I was the one helping. It was an awesome feeling.

DESIGN PRINCIPLE #1
What's Your "WHY?"

Wow, the perceptiveness of the teacher, coupled with your vulnerability and transparency makes that a great story. Now, let's talk about your first principle, What's Your WHY?

Henry: Let's take a step back so that I can tell you how I was brought into this world. It's actually funny, because when I was young my mother would call me her 'miracle baby," and tell this story to her girlfriends that it took her sixteen years to have me. Hearing that line over and over so many times made me think that it actually took a woman sixteen years to have a baby, not nine months. I never understood what she meant, until I got older and learned that my parents tried to have a baby fir sixteen years, but complications on both ends kept them from getting pregnant. Their refusal to give up on something they wanted so badly is a trait that has been instilled in me.

Now fast forward about eighteen months later. I was here, my parents were over the moon, and then one night, my mom came into my room to learn that I wasn't breathing. I was unresponsive, and blue in the face. The condition was called hyponatremia, which means that the level of sodium in my blood was abnormally low. My mom freaked out, called my father, and they immediately called 911. After time in the hospital, the doctor was able to raise my levels and I was ok. My mom told this story many times, and would preface it with the fact that she believed that I was put here for a reason. Sixteen years to have me, and then a near death experience at the age of two. Crazy.

As I've gotten older, I've really learned to appreciate life more, and try to treat each day as if it's my last. I know that sounds cliché, but there's a lot of truth to it. That's my WHY in a nutshell. It's probably no surprise that I took on that Special Events position at the hospital, which eventually morphed into me creating my own business, which morphed again into me helping others grow their businesses.

You went from helping kids in the fourth grade to helping other small business owners become entrepreneurs and find their WHY. But, is there a process to helping others discover this?

Henry: The biggest thing is, you need to know where you're going before you make that first step. We're going to tiptoe into principle number two, which is about having a vision, a little bit, but you need to map out where you want to be first and foremost. You need to envision it; then really picture it; you need to feel it, and then ask yourself "why do I want this.? That's how you create your WHY. It's really about planning with the end in mind. I knew that I wanted to help other small business owners achieve their goals—whatever that might be. My WHY for wanting that is that I feel as if I'm here on borrowed time because of my experiences at a young age, and want to make the best of every minute that I've got.

So you need to have a navigational point; kind of like how Stephen Covey said "begin with the end in mind." Then, once you have that compass pointed in the right direction, now you can create your story. What advice can you give about allowing the WHY to pull you in the right direction rather than push you towards something you may not be passionate about?

Henry: Great question. I feel like if it's not a "hell yes," then it's got to be a "hell no." I've learned that time is our most valuable asset and if we're not doing the things that we truly want to be doing do, then we're wasting our time. We're also wasting other people's time. The energy that leads you should always be a pulling force; almost magnetic. When you're pushed into something, you often feel obligated, or rushed. Not natural. For me, what's real is knowing that I am seeing the course for something that I want to do or accomplish. I'm very passionate about that.

So, when you're "pulled" you will often feel joy, clarity, calmness, overall good emotions, because your navigational compass has been set to the right "end goal?"

Henry: Exactly. You want those good feelings to flow freely. You don't want them to come as a result of being forced.

Let's shift gears a bit. I want to know why you think success comes easy for some people but not for others.

Henry: Here's what I think. Success comes easier to those who focus on their strengths and then delegate out their weaknesses. We get in our own way when we spend time on things that we aren't good at. It really comes down to being self-aware. If you know that you suck at X, Y, and Z, then hand those tasks over to someone who doesn't. You need to find a balance between trying new things and staying in your lane. That's why there are hierarchies in business, so that each person, or group of people can bring their best assets to the table.

Why do people live most of their lives wanting and wishing, as opposed to making progress toward an end goal?

Henry: Fear. We're so afraid of failing that we often paralyze ourselves. One of my mentors, Gary Vaynerchuk, tells a story about when he was in his early twenties how he would spend time with folks in their eighties and nineties and ask them what they would have wanted to do in the past that they didn't get a chance to do. Most of them would respond with so much regret, which made Gary really depressed. While many people spend their time wishing and waiting because of fear, I am motivated by the fear of regret. I don't want to be eighty thinking about what I could have done, or who I could have been. You must push through fear. Period. Ask yourself "what's the worst case scenario," and then keep moving.

DESIGN APPLICATION #1
What's Your "WHY?"

What's your story?

Henry M. Kaminski Jr.

What are you REALLY living for?

Henry M. Kaminski Jr.

What will pull you towards your WHY?

Henry M. Kaminski Jr.

DESIGN PRINCIPLE #2
Having a Vision

How does having a vision help determine your WHY?

Henry: I think having a clear vision, and knowing what you want to get out of life, as well as what you're living for, helps you achieve your goals more quickly. Did you ever hear the saying, "live life on purpose?" That's what it comes down to.

When I first started Unique Designz, I had a grandiose vision, which was that I was going to run my business on the top floor of a sick skyscraper in midtown Manhattan; floor-to-ceiling windows, about 20 graphic designers lined up in their stations and me walking up and down the aisles reviewing their work. I was going to be the "Commander in Chief" of my business.

While a lot of the things that I wanted to achieve have come to fruition, the reality is much different from the picture that I just painted. I always wanted to build a team, and while my team doesn't sit on the top floor of a building in midtown, they come from all walks of life, and levels ability and work remotely out of their homes.

So would it be fair to say that there may be slight pivots along the way?

Henry: Absolutely. What I had envisioned might have changed, or pivoted, but my end goal of building a team remained the same. When you reach a certain point in your business, you realize quickly that in order to get to the next level, you need to build a team. I was a one man show for so long, handling every facet of my business that I wasn't doing any of my tasks well.

When I finally learned to delegate out my weaknesses, I really started to thrive. My team is now an extension of my family, and I wouldn't be able to serve my clients the way that I do without them.

What the difference between a WHY and a vision or purpose?

Henry: A vision or purpose lets you see where you're going, whereas the WHY the reason for going there. You need to understand "WHY" you're doing something before you do it. It will set your purpose, and give you a clear and focused vision.

It's almost like you're visualizing your business (or personal) successes before they happen in a motivating way.

Henry: That's right. I had a conversation with my wife recently about this. We're recently celebrated our five-year wedding anniversary, and planned a vacation around it. While we were away, we talked about everything that we had accomplished since we got married, and realized that the things we didn't have a clear vision on didn't come to fruition, but that the things that we could see happened.

That's a really relevant proof of that principle. Doesn't that motivate you to work on really getting a better focus on the things that didn't happen?

Henry: Yea, and that's where the game changes. When you take the time, put in the work, and really make the effort, things happen.

So then once you've established an end goal, say for a client, you can start formulating the strategy, correct?

Henry: While that's usually how it works, sometimes you trip over things that you weren't expecting and realize that it's what you've been looking for. Kind of like a missing puzzle piece. That's what makes Entrepreneurship so fascinating.

Ok, so is it fair to say that if hadn't set a clear destination, you may have ignored that missing puzzle piece. Basically, you may have ignored what was right in front of you because you didn't have a clear sense of what it was that you wanted or where you were going?

Henry: That's it! Knowing the end game and not getting derailed by what I like to call "shiny object syndrome," will definitely help you stay the course.

DESIGN APPLICATION #2

Describe in detail, your WHY so that someone reading this can clearly visualize it.

_____
_____
_____
_____
_____
_____
_____
_____
_____
_____
_____
_____
_____
_____
_____
_____
_____

Henry M. Kaminski Jr.

DESIGN PRINCIPLE #3
Things Aren't Always What They Seem

Help us move from developing our "why", to clarifying our vision, to understanding that things aren't always what they seem.

Henry: This next principle is really important to understanding WHY you do the things you do day in- and day-out. When I first started Unique Designz, it was all about the money. I have an uncle who is an extremely successful business man; grew a business from nothing to $200 million dollars over the course of his career. Forty-five years of being in business, which was a great motivator for me. I saw a lot of the material things that came with my uncle's success, and I wanted the same things for my life. I wanted the car, the house, the watch. Everything that he had, I wanted. But then, as my business grew, and I was slowly able to get those "things," I realized that there was still something missing. I was only happy for about five minutes.
Then one day it hit me. Nobody gives a damn about what you have. They're more concerned with your WHY; your reason for doing things. They don't care what watch you're wearing or what car you drive; the only person who cares is you. But, if you

explain to someone WHY you do what you do, they will care about you. It's that simple.

So, in the early stages of growing my business, and coming into my own money, I got really into cars. What had made me feel good about myself slowly started to make me feel miserable. I admit, that at the time I wanted to impress people and prove to them that I did this on my own. But, the reality was that nobody cared. It got to a point that a family member shared that another family member actually said "Henry has to be a drug dealer, because there's no way he could drive *that* car designing business cards." It was like a knife through my heart. My own family resented the fact that I had achieved a level of success similar to theirs.

Looking back, I can now admit that I was pretty foolish to spend my money on things that I thought would not only impress others, but make me feel better. I'm at a point now where if it's not a "hell yes", then it's got to be a "hell no." Everything I do in my life now is for a much better WHY. My WHY is focused more on how I can help and serve others, not how I can impress others. I've also learned that the more I give, the more it comes back around to me in positive ways. I'm not expecting anything in return. It just kind of happens. I'm at a point now in business where I can be more selective about who I work with since it's no longer about the money. That's why it's so important to understand that things aren't always what they appear to be. Money has the potential to create a lot of smoke and mirrors; I've met a lot of successful people over the years who've had tons of money but nothing else going for them. I feel for those people. If you've had the chance to meet me, or to speak with me, and then follow me on social media, you will quickly learn that I'm no different. What you see is what you get with me, and I pride myself on that.

I read this one-liner that really hit me that said, "if you're not in business to help others, you will never be a profitable business." So true, because at one time I was only in business to make money and try to impress the people around me, and at the end of the day I wasn't profitable. My former mindset caused my business to slowly disintegrate, almost to nothing, until I smartened up and got the help and got my mind in the right place to turn it all around and take it to where it is today. It got to a point that I was negative $2500 in my bank account, and a wife who was on the verge of divorcing me because of the way that I was treating her and the people around us. It finally hit me that if I kept going in the direction that I was headed, I was going to lose it all.

I smartened up and invested in coaching program under the direction of Russell Brunson, founder of ClickFunnels.com. I remember our first conference call like it was yesterday. I told him my story, and by the end of the call, we were literally both balling our eyes out. I told him that I had just given him $10,000 that I didn't have and that his coaching program HAD to work. There was no other option. Russell started coaching me on how to get my personal story out there, and that's when things started to change for the better...

Would you say that the pivot was more internal at first, and if so, at what point did the changes that you were making start to be apparent to the people around you?

Henry: The pivot was actually external, because I kept hearing the voices of the people closest to me in my ear telling me that something had to change. Internally, I knew that was something that I didn't want to happen, so I quickly made the change. I knew that if I didn't, the people around me who I cared about, but had taken advantage of for so long, were going to leave me.

The coaching that I received from Russell's camp essentially "rewired" me to be more selfless and to put others before myself. I immediately started implementing the coaching that I received and literally within six weeks, I made back the $10,000 that I had invested in Russell's coaching program.

Fast forward to today, and, I think about how much my business has grown and matured, and how much revenue I've gained from shifting my mindset. I sometimes still can't believe it. For the past 16 months, I've had my head down just grinding it out. Now I finally have the confidence to say "I got this!" This time around I'm going to be smarter about it and not make the same mistakes that I did in the past. I started getting my personality out there more and more because I realized that people want to do business with people.

I imagine that you had to be 100% genuine throughout this process so that people didn't get the wrong idea as to why you were making this pivot. Can you pinpoint the exact moment when you knew that you had to make a change?

Henry: Yeah, sure. I used to spend 12-14 hours a day working and my wife didn't see me until I got into bed around one in the morning, and she had already been asleep two-three hours. I did that for the first three years of our marriage, and then things really started to hit the fan. She told me how unhappy she was, and it was at that moment that I decided to shift my focus to my family. I needed to be more present, because in that moment I wasn't present at all. I was so afraid of losing my wife that I slowly started to "unplug" around five or six o'clock so that I could spend time with her more regularly. It all comes back to the WHY. Why do I unplug at five o'clock? Because I want to spend more time with the people who mean the most to me.

I've learned that setting expectations and being true to your word builds a tremendous amount of trust. It took a while for my wife to trust that I was serious about changing my life for the better, but I was determined to prove to her that I could stay true to my word.

You mentioned having role models. But, did you ever come to find that the person who you looked up to wasn't what they appeared to be on the surface? How did you deal with that disappointment, and then how do you bounce back from it?

Henry: When that happened to me, I tried hard to pull the positives out of the situation. Rather than resenting that person, or putting them down, I identified what I didn't want to do in my own life. Listen, whatever happened to that person happened to them because of decisions that they made-not because of anything that I did. It's ok to separate yourself from people who no longer bring value to your life, so I guess the biggest takeaway for me would be to focus on the positive, and not the negative and to move forward from that. What's most important is how happy you are; to me, that's what measures whether you're living a wealthy life. When it comes to building your business, I've learned that money is just there to keep score. I say that after years of being coached and mentored, and learning to understand what really matters. It took time, but I got there, and I now want to help other like-minded business owners do the same.

Henry M. Kaminski Jr.

DESIGN APPLICATION #3

First, describe your definition of success, and then explain how it can be measured.

_____
_____
_____
_____
_____
_____
_____
_____
_____
_____
_____
_____
_____
_____
_____
_____

Refuse to Give Up

Now, describe three challenges that you currently face in your business and/or personal life.

_____
_____
_____
_____
_____
_____
_____
_____
_____
_____
_____
_____
_____
_____
_____
_____
_____
_____
_____
_____

Refuse to Give Up

Next, select <u>one</u> challenge and explain what you could do to overcome it.

_____
_____
_____
_____
_____
_____
_____
_____
_____
_____
_____
_____
_____
_____
_____
_____
_____
_____
_____
_____

Refuse to Give Up

Finally, explain WHY it's important for you to overcome this particular challenge.

Refuse to Give Up

DESIGN PRINCIPLE #4
Building Relationships

Now that we've gotten through three of your four principles, can you share how to start moving towards building relationships?

Henry: I read somewhere that you should "serve first, ask later." Gary Vaynerchuk, who I referenced earlier as being a mentor- someone who I follow- often says to give 51% in a partnership, because that's how you build strong relationships. By giving more than 50%, you are showing a true commitment to whatever it is you are working on. Another thing is not to be afraid to get around people who know more than you. I had always wanted to be that "big fish" in a small pond, until I realized that being in that position wasn't letting me grow, or learn or even fail at anything, because I essentially knew everything. I was able to take Unique Designz to the next level once I surrounded myself with people who could teach me a thing or two. You need to get around real players who have had real results. That's it.

Business owners and entrepreneurs who have worked hard to grow their business the same way I did are the people who draw my attention. Build relationships with people who are committed to their work and actually able to achieve results similar to the ones that you want to achieve.

You've alluded to the importance of relationship-building both personally and professionally throughout this interview, but what does a healthy business relationship look like in your mind?

Henry: First and foremost, you want your values to align with your partner; you want to make sure you guys are on the "same page." Next, whatever partnership you create must have the potential to be a "win-win" situation for everyone. Goals, expectations, roles, and responsibilities must be agreed upon up front, because the minute one person feels as if they are doing more-saying more than the other, the partnership will become imbalanced.

I struggled for a long time with how to provide value to my customers. I was able to create a kick-ass marketing materials, but unable to help grow my client's revenue beyond that one-off campaign. I was finally able to partner up with a guy who had done business development for small business-and turning them into major franchises in a very short period of time; he was even featured in Entrepreneur Magazine. I didn't have that kind of

It probably would have taken me years to gain that level of experience. Now, I am able to help clients grow their businesses beyond that one-time marketing campaign; they are repeat customers-almost like mini partnerships in their own way, because I have an authority on my team who can help them strategically in a way that I couldn't.

What are some tactics for nurturing a business relationship once it's been established?

Henry: Integrity is a big one. If you say something or put something out there, you must act on it. It's basically the law of reciprocity; what you give will come back around in a positive way. I think I mentioned that earlier, but it's really important. I'm not saying to do something to get something back in return, but when you do something positive, you will eventually see it come back around-and often in an unexpected way. We do business with people to keep that reciprocity moving. Another way to nurture a relationship is to be transparent. Be open with your partner, even if that means sharing information that they may not agree with or may not want to hear. I get mad at my wife sometimes because she is extremely transparent. What you see is what you get with her, and she makes no apologies for it. But, because of that I know that I can trust her explicitly. It should be the same in business.

Would you say that relationship-building is on par with determining your WHY?

Henry: Yes. In most cases, you won't be able to achieve your WHY in business without the help of others. You can't be everything to everyone, and you aren't going to be good at

everything, which is why building and then nurturing strong business relationships is so important. Surround yourself with people who know more than you, who have a vested interest in helping you grow your business so that you can take your business to the next level.

By successfully addressing these four principles, what outcome could someone hope to achieve?

Henry: My hope is that by following these four principles, you will:
1. Have a clear vision of where you want to go;
2. Understand WHY you're doing what you're doing;
3. See things for what they truly are; and
4. Build relationships that serve you and enable you to take your business to the next level

These principles helped shift my mindset and make me feel more fulfilled, and I truly hope they do the same for you.

OK, now that we've identified these four principles, as well as some of the obstacles that you faced while trying to live these principles, what's the solution?

Henry: Get out there and make things happen. You have the tools, so start building. I think if we all just took five minutes at the beginning and end of our day to reflect on what happened over the course of the day, we would be more mindful of where we needed to go when we wake up the next morning. I use a journal to record what made my day awesome, and what could have made it better. I keep it on my nightstand and use it when I wake up in the morning and when I go to bed at night, and it's helped me implement these principles. I don't think people take the time to pre-plan their day and what they want to get out of it, which is why the journal really helps.

What might some consequences be for someone who understands these principles, but chooses not to follow them?

Henry: All I can say is that you're only fooling yourself if you choose not to follow these pretty simple steps. Nothing that I've shared is a new discovery-but it was my discovery and these steps are what helped me grow my business, so why not allow it to do the same for you?

What's one more piece of advice that you can give to someone who might be at a crossroads in either the business or personal life?

Henry: Listen to your gut, because it's very telling. If you aren't feeling it, then don't act on it. If you think you need help, then ask for it. I didn't always do this and it only pushed me farther from my goals. Don't weigh a business decision based on fear, or how much work it might involve, but rather how it's going to serve you now as well as in the long term.

I hope you've found tremendous value out of the accomplishments and the mistakes that I've made on my entrepreneurial journey.

DESIGN APPLICATION #4

Describe one relationship that you've built and explain how it serves you in growing your business.

_____
_____
_____
_____
_____
_____
_____
_____
_____
_____
_____
_____
_____
_____
_____
_____
_____

Henry M. Kaminski Jr.

Now, describe one relationship that you've had that did not serve you well in business, and explain what you did about it.

_____
_____
_____
_____
_____
_____
_____
_____
_____
_____
_____
_____
_____
_____
_____
_____
_____
_____

Henry M. Kaminski Jr.

Do you consider yourself to be transparent in business? If so, how, and if not, why?

_____
_____
_____
_____
_____
_____
_____
_____
_____
_____
_____
_____
_____
_____
_____
_____
_____
_____

Finally, what made today awesome, and what are some areas that you could have improved upon both personally and professionally?

___

___

___

___

___

___

___

___

___

___

___

___

___

___

___

___

___

___

Henry M. Kaminski Jr.

Refuse to Give Up

Connect with Henry

Web:	www.uniquedesignz.net
YouTube:	Unique Designz by the HMK Group
Instagram:	Unique_Designz
Email	info@uniquedesignz.net
Partner Site:	www.HowToMonetize.net

www.ingramcontent.com/pod-product-compliance
Lightning Source LLC
Chambersburg PA
CBHW070356190526
45169CB00003B/1032